"I THINK THE BIGGEST DISEASE THIS
WORLD SUFFERS FROM . . . IS THE DISEASE
OF PEOPLE FEELING UNLOVED, AND I KNOW
THAT I CAN GIVE LOVE."

DIANA

1961–1997

ABDO
Publishing Company

DIANA

THE PEOPLE'S PRINCESS

BY LISA OWINGS

CREDITS

Published by ABDO Publishing Company, PO Box 398166, Minneapolis, MN 55439. Copyright © 2013 by Abdo Consulting Group, Inc. International copyrights reserved in all countries. No part of this book may be reproduced in any form without written permission from the publisher. The Essential Library™ is a trademark and logo of ABDO Publishing Company.

Printed in the United States of America,
North Mankato, Minnesota
062012
092012

 THIS BOOK CONTAINS AT LEAST 10% RECYCLED MATERIALS.

Editor: Melissa York
Series Designer: Becky Daum

Library of Congress Cataloging-in-Publication Data
Owings, Lisa.
   Diana : the People's Princess / Lisa Owings.
       p. cm. -- (Lives cut short)
   Includes bibliographical references.
   ISBN 978-1-61783-545-2
   1. Diana, Princess of Wales, 1961-1997--Juvenile literature.
2. Princesses--Great Britain--Biography--Juvenile literature. I. Title.
   DA591.A45D535523 2012
   941.085092--dc23
   [B]
                                          2012018441

TABLE OF CONTENTS

1

THE FAIRY TALE

It was the evening of July 28, 1981. Outside the walls of Buckingham Palace, the world buzzed with excitement. Inside, Lady Diana Spencer was thinking about what her life would be like when she became Princess of Wales after marrying Prince Charles the next day. The 19-year-old came from a noble family. She had grown up alongside royalty, often playing with young Princes Andrew and Edward, the brothers of her fiancé. But palace life was not what she expected. Diana felt unsure of herself

▶ DIANA SPENCER AND PRINCE CHARLES ANNOUNCED THEIR ENGAGEMENT ON FEBRUARY 24, 1981.

in this world of excess and ritual. Over the five and a half months since the engagement, the royal family was kind to her but distant. She was lonely more often than not. But these challenges were not enough to stop a woman in love from becoming a princess. Diana felt she could handle anything as long as Prince Charles was at her side.

The princess-to-be was giddy with excitement in the months leading up to the wedding. She dined with the queen, shopped for clothes, enjoyed dance lessons, and swam in the palace pool. Photographers followed her to the lavish events she attended. Staff members were available to meet her every need. The British people already adored her. Yet at times, Diana doubted she could live up to her people's expectations.

Naturally shy, Diana now felt the strain of always being in the spotlight. All eyes were on her as the British people watched the woman who could one day become their queen. As a result of this attention, Diana became painfully conscious of her public image. She began losing weight so quickly that many were concerned about her health. Things only got worse when Diana grew suspicious that her fiancé had romantic feelings for another woman: Camilla Parker Bowles. Diana wrote letters to her friends to vent her doubt and frustration. But she knew she had to continue on the path she had chosen. As her sister would remind her just before the wedding, "Your face is on the tea towels, so you're too late to chicken out."[1]

Diana occupied herself with preparations as the wedding date drew closer. In true princess style, Diana chose the wedding dress of her dreams. She hired David and Elizabeth Emanuel to design the dress. It had to be romantic enough for Diana and dramatic enough for the rest of the world. The trio decided on a ruffled confection of silk, lace, and pearls. The dress would have enormous sleeves, a fitted waist, and a full skirt. Its most memorable feature would be the extravagant 25-foot (8 m) train. Diana's rapid weight loss made fittings a struggle. Dragging so much fabric around was also a challenge. But after much altering, arranging, and rehearsing, everything was ready for the wedding.

Diana's Eating Disorder

Diana suffered from bulimia for several years. Her struggle with this eating disorder began just after her engagement on February 6, 1981. It started when Prince Charles made a remark about her weight. "Oh, a bit chubby here, aren't we?" he reportedly asked.[2] Diana began eating large quantities of food to comfort herself. Then she would make herself throw up. In the months leading up to the wedding, Diana became dangerously thin. The disorder continued to plague her until a few years before her death.

A HAPPY BEGINNING

The night before the wedding, people began setting up camp around the palace, the church, and the streets between to secure the best views of the newest royal couple. The cheers of the spectators were accompanied by the booming of fireworks. Diana spent a restless night away from her prince. Charles's words of encouragement replayed in her mind: "I'm so proud of you, and when you come up I'll be there at the altar for you

The Dress

Lady Diana first heard of the Emanuels when she asked who had made a romantic blouse she particularly liked. The husband-and-wife team also designed the black dress Diana wore to her first formal event after becoming engaged to the prince. Its low neckline, paired with the fact that royals traditionally wore black only to funerals, helped the future princess make headlines. However unconventional, no one could deny how glamorous Diana looked that evening.

The Emanuels had to take drastic measures to keep Diana's wedding dress a secret. Under constant surveillance by journalists, the designers kept their windows closed for months. The Emanuels kept the dress locked in a safe when they were not working on it. Two security guards protected the gown at night.

The dress was a huge undertaking. The Emanuels painstakingly sewed more than 10,000 pearls and sequins onto 45 feet (14 m) of locally spun silk taffeta. Also stitched inside the dress was a gold horseshoe charm for luck. The Emanuels even made a second wedding dress in case the first one was revealed before the big day.

▲ THE EMANUELS WORKED ON DIANA'S WEDDING DRESS
IN SECRET.

tomorrow. Just look 'em in the eye and knock
'em dead."[3]

Early on the morning of July 29, 1981, Lady
Diana began her transformation. She watched
news coverage of herself on the television in her
dressing room while her bridesmaids fluttered
around her. With a diamond tiara pinned to her
head but still wearing jeans, Diana sat through
hair and makeup. Then the Emanuels put the
dress on her and made some final adjustments.
Finally, Diana pulled her long veil into place.

A sparkling glass carriage was waiting. It took
the efforts of all of Diana's attendants to get both

bride and dress inside. Diana's father, Edward "Johnnie" Spencer, rode with her to Saint Paul's Cathedral. He was bursting with pride and waved to the crowds enthusiastically all the way to the church.

Whistles and cheers from the massive crowd marked Diana's arrival at the cathedral. The noise reached its peak as Diana stepped out of her carriage. As trumpets sounded a bright fanfare, Diana climbed the steps to the church and took her father's arm. Then the two began their long, slow walk down the aisle. Music played and the 3,500 guests in the cathedral watched quietly and respectfully for the three and a half minutes it took for Diana to reach the altar. When she arrived, Prince Charles leaned toward his bride to whisper, "You look wonderful." Diana shyly replied, "Wonderful for you."[4]

The wedding ceremony lasted more than an hour, but it was all a happy blur. The Prince and Princess of Wales stumbled through their vows, making minor mistakes in the formal wording. However, Diana's formal curtsy to the

The World Was Watching

Diana's wedding to Prince Charles was a spectacle not to be missed. Approximately 750 million pairs of eyes were glued to television sets across the globe as Diana walked down the aisle. According to the British Broadcasting Corporation (BBC), the royal wedding was the most popular television event in history.

▲ DIANA AND PRINCE CHARLES GREETED THE CROWDS
AFTER THEIR WEDDING.

queen was graceful despite her heavy dress. The
royal couple sealed their future together with a
kiss.

Later, the couple appeared on the balcony
outside Buckingham Palace, and the ecstatic
crowd welcomed them by demanding more
kisses. The couple delivered, and as Princess
Diana stood with her husband before masses
of adoring fans, she was filled with hope for
the future. And yet, deep down, Diana knew
everything was not perfect, and she sensed she
would never become queen.

———•◆•———

2

BECOMING A LADY

Diana Frances Spencer was born into a world of lords and ladies on July 1, 1961, and her family had a close relationship with the British royal family. Diana's parents, Johnnie and Frances Spencer, held the title Lord and Lady Althorp. Diana's early life was charmed in many ways. She grew up in Park House, a ten-bedroom mansion in the English countryside. The Spencers' home was owned by the queen and situated on her Sandringham Estate, where the royal family came to spend holidays in the country.

▶ DIANA WAS BORN INTO AN ANCIENT NOBLE FAMILY.

Park House was a picturesque setting for Diana's early years. The sea was just a few miles away, and the Spencer family often enjoyed trips to the beach. Diana also began showing her athleticism in the swimming pool and on the tennis court at Park House.

Even as a young girl, Diana impressed those close to her with her compassionate and nurturing spirit. She cared for hamsters, guinea pigs, rabbits, dogs, ponies, and a cat named Marmalade. To Diana, these animals were more than just pets and playthings. Horses were the only creatures she did not express fondness for. She had taken a bad fall while learning to ride, and it made her fearful of them.

MONEY CANNOT BUY HAPPINESS

Diana adored her parents, but they were distant, leaving their children in the care of nannies and governesses. Diana also struggled with the knowledge that her parents had hoped their third child would be a boy. She could not help feeling like a disappointment. Diana looked up to her two older sisters, Sarah and Jane, who were six and four years older than Diana, respectively. However, the age difference between Diana and her sisters made her feel separate. Her brother,

▲ DIANA AND HER BROTHER, CHARLES, IN 1968

Charles, three years younger than Diana, was her closest childhood companion.

When Diana was six years old, Sarah and Jane went to boarding school and henceforth returned home only on weekends and holidays. Johnnie and Frances began fighting more often. Their divorce in 1969 had a profound impact on their children—especially Diana and Charles, who still lived at home. Frances moved out and soon remarried. Though the children were fond of their new stepfather, they disliked being shuffled between their parents, and they felt alienated at school.

BREAKING AWAY

Diana's parents sent her to Riddlesworth Hall, a boarding school for girls, in 1970. She was nine years old. At first, Diana felt this was a punishment. However, she soon made friends with her classmates and began having fun at school.

Diana never excelled in academics, but she had an intelligence that went beyond books. She had an exceptional ability to sense other people's needs and emotions. Her teachers admired how eager she was to be helpful. They also noticed how she took her classmates under her wing and immediately put them at ease.

The headmistress of Riddlesworth noticed Diana's caring nature and

"You can be very bright and not interested in academia and still be sharp. That was Diana."[1]
—Reverend Sweet, Latin teacher and chaplain at Riddlesworth

awarded her the Legatt Cup for helpfulness. This acknowledgment helped Diana define herself not as the disappointing daughter of divorced parents but as an individual who could make a difference in people's lives.

WEST HEATH

When she was 12, Diana joined Jane at another boarding school for girls called West Heath. Rebellious behavior had gotten her oldest sister, Sarah, expelled from the school in 1971. Diana had a mischievous streak of her own as a teenager. She was popular and, though she was sometimes shy in class, she tended to be rowdy with her friends. She continued with

Life at Riddlesworth

Being at Riddlesworth seemed to help Diana gain self-confidence. Although she struggled in class, she found herself in the perfect environment to explore her other talents. She threw herself into sports and was an especially gifted swimmer and dancer. She also participated in school plays, though she always refused speaking parts.

One thing Diana liked about Riddlesworth was she was able to bring her pet guinea pig. Diana quickly took over responsibility for Pets' Corner, where the students' pets were kept. "Diana organized the sweeping rotations and all that kind of thing—she was Queen of Pets' Corner at one stage," recalled headmistress Patricia Wood.[2] Diana later said of that time, "I won all sorts of prizes for best-kept guinea pig, but in the academic department you might as well forget that."[3]

▲ DIANA SPENT MOST OF HER FORMATIVE YEARS AT BOARDING SCHOOL.

swimming and tennis and was especially passionate about ballet.

West Heath encouraged its students to volunteer, and Diana became active in her community. Penny Walker, Diana's teacher at West Heath, remembered her student's willingness to help others:

> She went to the local mental hospital, Darenth Park. We also used to have parties for the elderly at West Heath, and she was always a big part of that. She didn't have to do it; it was by choice.[4]

Walker also placed special trust in Diana by letting the teenager babysit her newborn. Diana was a natural with children. It became clear she was more interested in people than schoolwork. However, Walker was not alone in her belief that "she was one of the smartest girls in my class."[5]

LADY DIANA

In 1975, two years after Diana went to West Heath, her grandfather died unexpectedly. He had been the seventh Earl of Spencer, and Diana's father inherited the title to become the eighth earl. The new Earl of Spencer also inherited his father's home in Althorp. Diana's family quickly moved into the sprawling residence situated on 14,000 acres (5,700 ha). It was a much more formal place than Park House, with 121 rooms

In the United Kingdom, noble titles are inherited through families. The head of Diana's family is the Earl of Spencer. An earl is a middle rank of the nobility, below a duke and a marquess but above a viscount and a baron. Diana's grandfather was the seventh Earl of Spencer, her father was the eighth, and her brother became the ninth Earl of Spencer in 1992. Other members of the family hold other titles. Diana's parents were a viscount and countess, called Lord and Lady Althorp, before Diana's father became earl. At that time, Diana's brother became Viscount Althorp, and Diana and her sisters were granted the courtesy title "lady."

and portraits of the Spencer family's ancestors covering the walls.

Diana faced another major change the summer she turned 14. There was a new woman in her father's life: Raine, Countess of Dartmouth. All of the Spencer children strongly disliked her. "We thought she was going to take Daddy away from us," Diana explained.[6] However, Johnnie married her in 1976.

Living at Althorp and having an earl for a father did have its perks, though. Diana and her siblings became lords and ladies. Additionally, Diana would meet her future husband at the Althorp estate.

▲ DIANA'S FAMILY'S ESTATE, ALTHORP

3

MEETING PRINCE CHARMING

When Diana met Prince Charles in November 1977, it was far from love at first sight. Diana was 16 years old. Prince Charles was dating her 22-year-old sister. Sarah had invited the prince to Althorp for some shooting practice. Diana had the weekend off from school and was home to meet him.

Prince Charles seemed enchanted by Diana. Something about her often drew people in. After dinner that first night, the prince asked Diana to give him a tour of the art gallery at Althorp.

▶ DIANA MATURED QUICKLY THROUGH HER TEEN YEARS.

But jealous Sarah was not about to give her sister the pleasure, and she conducted the tour herself. Diana had no intention of stealing her sister's man—at the time, she even found Prince Charles depressing. Nonetheless, Diana and Prince Charles had other opportunities to get to know each other that weekend. Prince Charles came away thinking Diana was "very jolly and amusing and attractive."[1] And Diana must have formed a better opinion of him, too, because she could not stop talking about him when she got back to West Heath.

AFTER SCHOOL

In 1978, Diana left West Heath to attend a private school in Switzerland. However, she felt out of place there and did not feel the cost of tuition was worth it. Diana returned to England after just one term. That spring, Diana was a bridesmaid in Jane's wedding. Her sister married Robert Fellowes, who would later become the queen's assistant private secretary. Sarah's romance with Charles soon fizzled. But Diana was not daydreaming about marrying the prince in her sister's place. She was busy trying to find a job.

Diana felt ready to make her own way in the world at age 17, even though her parents did not think she was ready. But Diana would not be satisfied until she could be surrounded by the glamour of London. After months of begging, her parents gave in and allowed her to move into a London flat with two of her friends. Even though her mother owned the flat, Diana was expected to work. She cobbled together a full-time schedule out of several part-time jobs. She worked as a nanny, housekeeper, and cook for people within her social circle, including Sarah.

A Woman's Intuition

Diana seemed to have an uncanny ability to sense what would happen in the future. She was staying with a friend when her father had his stroke. Just before she learned what had happened, she had a frightening premonition. Someone had asked how her father was doing. To the surprise of everyone in the room, Diana responded, "I've got this strange feeling that he's going to drop down and if he dies, he'll die immediately, otherwise he'll survive."[2] It was not the first—nor the last—time Diana's intuition would be proven right.

TAKING THE BAD WITH THE GOOD

In September 1978, Diana's father suffered a life-threatening stroke and fell into a coma, though he later recovered. It was a difficult time, and Raine and the children fought constantly. Prince Charles's thirtieth birthday party in November was just the thing to raise Diana's spirits, but she was worried that Sarah, who was also invited, would not want her to attend. However, Sarah put aside any jealous feelings, and the sisters danced the night away at Buckingham Palace.

Diana enjoyed the evening, but it would not become clear until later that Prince Charles enjoyed her presence as well.

After the ball, Diana's mother helped her daughter get a position as a ballet teacher. This was a dream come true for Diana. However, similar to many of Diana's dreams, this one was not to last. A ski trip in the spring of 1979 was cut short when Diana fell and seriously injured her ankle. The dance studio was forced to hire a replacement teacher before Diana had fully recovered. However, Diana took the disappointment in stride.

For her eighteenth birthday, Diana's parents bought her a luxurious apartment of her own. She proudly decorated her new place and invited three of her closest friends to live with her. Diana's luck continued when she was hired as a part-time kindergarten teacher. Her students adored her. "[Diana] had a wonderful sense of humor and made [the children] laugh," recalled Kay King, who ran the school.[3]

DESTINED FOR ROYALTY

Throughout her adolescence, Diana felt she was destined for greatness. She did not know exactly what her future held, but whatever it was, she was determined to be prepared for it. This instinct

▲ DIANA OWNED AN APARTMENT IN THIS LONDON BUILDING.

kept her from getting too attached to any of the men she dated. "I knew I had to keep myself very tidy for whatever came my way," she said, meaning she wanted to avoid romantic entanglements that might cause a scandal later.[4]

Diana's destiny began falling into place at the end of 1979. She was invited to spend a weekend at Sandringham in February 1980, and she eagerly accepted. When a friend hinted the weekend might be the start of a romance with Prince Charles, Diana brushed the thought aside. She spent the weekend enjoying the elegant company, but she was still in awe of Prince Charles and focused little of her attention on him. However, Diana's next encounter with the prince would prove her friend right.

Prince Charles, who was then 31 years old, was aware of his duty to choose a bride and produce an heir to the throne. In July 1980, Prince Charles's thoughts returned to innocent, cheerful, 19-year-old Diana. She was invited to the home of some friends of the royal family. Prince Charles would be staying there for the weekend, and Diana would make an amusing companion.

When Diana and the prince got a moment alone, she was caught off guard by how interested he seemed in her. Diana secured her admirer's affection by revealing her compassionate nature. Prince Charles's mentor and closest friend, Lord Mountbatten, had recently been killed. The loss deeply affected the prince, and he was not sure how he would cope without this guiding force in his life. Diana took the opportunity to express her sympathy, saying,

> You looked so sad when you walked up the aisle at Lord Mountbatten's funeral. It was the most tragic thing I've ever seen. My heart bled for you when I watched. I thought, "It's wrong; you're lonely—you should be with somebody to look after you."[6]

Prince Charles was clearly moved. Word was already spreading that Diana might be the woman Prince Charles—along with the rest of the country—had been waiting for.

WHIRLWIND ROMANCE

The two went on another date in July, and Diana was now sure of the prince's interest in her. She was also becoming aware of how quickly her feelings for him were developing. In August, the couple enjoyed boat races from the deck of the *Britannia*, the royal yacht. In September, Diana was invited to join the prince at Balmoral. This castle in the hills of Scotland had long been a favorite retreat for the royal family. It had also become known as a place to test the suitability of potential princesses in the relative privacy of the castle. Diana was terrified of making a wrong move while at Balmoral and falling out of favor with the royal family. She was glad her sister Jane would be there to lend her support.

Prince Charles did his best to make Diana feel comfortable. Diana later recalled, "Charles used to ring me up and say, 'Would you like to come for a walk, come for a barbecue?' . . . I thought this was all wonderful."[7] Charles's friends were impressed by Diana's easygoing nature and willingness to join in the hunting and fishing activities. One of them noted,

> We went [hiking] together . . . she fell into a bog, she got covered in mud, laughed her head off . . . she was a sort of wonderful English schoolgirl who was game for anything.[8]

Diana had passed the Balmoral test.

MEET THE PRESS

The press had followed the prince to Balmoral in hopes of discovering his girlfriend's identity. They found Prince Charles casting his fishing line into the river that runs past Balmoral. Diana sat by his side. As soon as the couple noticed they had company, Diana hid behind a tree to prevent them from getting a photograph. Then she pulled out a pocket mirror so she could keep an eye on them. Journalist James Whitaker fondly remembers the face-off: "What a cunning lady, I thought. . . . [She] had to be a real professional to think of using a mirror to watch us watching her."[9]

From then on, Diana was constantly followed by the press. Photographers

Sneak Peek

Diana had to learn to deal with the press early in her relationship with Prince Charles. She put on a brave face in public, and few ever heard an unkind word slip past her lips. In private, though, the teenager shed countless tears, begged the royal family to step in, and devised ways to avoid or mislead the press.

Even though she acted poised in front of the camera, her interactions with the press were not always smooth. When a group of photographers showed up at her kindergarten, she decided to give them what they wanted in hopes they would leave her alone. Diana posed for a few pictures with the children. She looked youthful and pretty in a vest and lightweight skirt. The sun shone brightly behind her. When the photos were published, Diana was mortified. The skirt was see-through. But everyone agreed she was beautiful.

▲ THE PRESS BEGAN FOLLOWING DIANA EVERYWHERE
ONCE IT WAS CLEAR SHE AND CHARLES WERE DATING.

mobbed her apartment and the kindergarten
where she worked. Her phone rang until the
wee hours of the morning. She could not run
an errand or go for a walk without a crowd of
photographers following her. She used her car

as a decoy, found alternative entrances and exits, and arranged secret meetings with the prince. Her friends found it a fun game. For Diana, it was just one more obstacle to overcome as she and Charles grew closer.

———•◆•———

4

DIANA, PRINCESS OF WALES

The media was not the only source of pressure on the royal romance. Everyone sensed the relationship was nearing a critical point. Prince Charles, as heir to the throne, had to decide if Lady Diana could fill the role of wife, mother, and future queen of England. Diana had to decide if she was willing to face the challenges of royal life to be with the man she loved.

Most of Diana's friends and family could hardly wait for her engagement to the prince. However, her grandmother hinted Diana would

▶ BY THE END OF 1980, DIANA WAS APPEARING AT MORE ROYAL FUNCTIONS, INCLUDING PRINCESS MARGARET'S BIRTHDAY PARTY IN NOVEMBER.

always be an outsider at Buckingham Palace. "I don't think [the royal lifestyle] will suit you," she said.[1] Additionally, Diana had her own suspicions about Prince Charles's ex-girlfriend, Camilla Parker Bowles. Parker Bowles and the prince were obviously close—perhaps too close. But Diana believed her love for the prince was stronger than her doubts.

THE PROPOSAL

Early in 1981, the prince went on a ski trip to Switzerland to clear his head and relax with friends. He asked Diana to meet him at Windsor Castle on Friday, February 6. When she arrived that evening, he told her how much he had missed her. Then

The Other Woman

Prince Charles met Camilla Rosemary Shand in 1970. Their relationship became serious, but when the prince failed to propose, Camilla married Andrew Parker Bowles in 1973 and became Camilla Parker Bowles. Prince Charles and Camilla remained friends and resumed their romance in the late 1980s.

Throughout Diana's engagement to Prince Charles, she saw signs of Charles's and Parker Bowles's devotion to one another. He had an intimate phone conversation with her before he left for Australia. On another occasion, Diana overheard him tell Parker Bowles, "Whatever happens, I will always love you."[2] Just before the wedding, he had a bracelet made for Parker Bowles. According to rumor, it featured the entwined initials of their nicknames for each other. On Diana and Charles's honeymoon, the prince wore cufflinks Parker Bowles had given him. Charles later admitted to an affair with Parker Bowles starting in 1986. They married in 2005.

he asked, "Will you marry me?"[3] Wanting to prevent an impulsive answer, he also reminded her of the responsibility she would take on by accepting his proposal. Diana could not hide her nerves, and a girlish giggle bubbled out. But she had been waiting for this moment. Diana said yes and told Prince Charles how much she loved him.

After the Proposal

After the prince proposed, Diana returned to her apartment to share her excitement with her room-mates. Her friends were thrilled, and they took Diana on a joyride around the city. The next morn-ing, Diana made phone call after phone call. Everyone in her family was happy for her. When she told her brother, Charles, she was getting married, he joked, "Who to?"[4]

Diana was ecstatic, and so were her friends and family. However, Diana would have to wait to share her happiness with the rest of the world. Prince Charles wanted to give Diana a few weeks to process her decision and be absolutely sure this was what she wanted. The engagement was to be kept secret until the official announcement on February 24. In the meantime, Diana flew to Australia with her mother to reflect, relax, and begin planning the wedding.

THE ANNOUNCEMENT

Diana returned home two days before she and Prince Charles were scheduled to share their good news with the public. The weeks away from her fiancé had turned some of Diana's excitement into anxiety. The prince had not contacted her even once while she was gone. To add to her worries, she was to move into Clarence House, first as a guest and then as a permanent resident after the engagement was announced. Clarence House is one of the royal family's luxurious residences. It stands just a ten-minute walk from Buckingham Palace. Despite these worries, 19-year-old Diana looked forward to what lay ahead. She would soon marry the man she loved. She also knew she could use her position as princess to help others in new ways.

For the big reveal on February 24, Diana wore a blue suit and, for the first time in public, her large sapphire-and-diamond engagement ring. The couple smiled for photos in front of Buckingham Palace. Then they nervously answered questions for a television interview. The couple appeared happy and affectionate with one another, though Charles seemed a little stiff and uncomfortable. When the interviewer asked if they were in love, Diana immediately replied, "Of course!" She was noticeably crushed when the prince added, "Whatever 'in love' means."[5]

▲ Queen Elizabeth gave her formal consent for the marriage on March 27, 1981.

Trial by Fire

Prince Charles's lukewarm response probably did little to give Diana the confidence she needed to face the changes ahead. Still, she was hopeful their relationship was solid. Soon after the engagement was announced, Diana moved into Clarence House officially. The move marked the end of Diana's private life. From then on, her life and image would be carefully managed by the royal family and closely scrutinized by the public.

▲ DIANA MET PARKER BOWLES ON SEVERAL OCCASIONS EARLY IN HER RELATIONSHIP WITH CHARLES.

Diana felt isolated. "I couldn't believe how cold everyone was [at the palace]," she later said.[6]

About a month after the official engagement, Charles left Diana to fend for herself and plan the wedding while he toured Australia and New Zealand. In Charles's absence, Parker Bowles saw an opportunity. She invited Diana to lunch, and Diana naively accepted. She later realized the other woman had been sizing her up, trying to gauge how much of a threat she posed to Parker Bowles's relationship with the prince. "I was so immature, I didn't know about jealousy [at the time]," said Diana.[7]

A lack of companionship, unfamiliarity with royal protocol, changing living arrangements, and growing suspicions of Parker Bowles often overshadowed Diana's excitement before the wedding. The attention of the press made her life even more challenging. Under such stress, Diana's bulimia took a firm hold. Yet Diana believed her troubles would more or less end when she and the prince were married.

THE HONEYMOON

The big day was July 29, 1981, and the huge event went off almost perfectly. After the wedding, Diana and Charles embarked on their Mediterranean honeymoon cruise aboard the royal yacht. Diana felt relieved now that she was officially Prince Charles's wife. She looked forward to a relaxing vacation with her husband, away from the public eye.

Diana later claimed her honeymoon was anything but relaxing and private. She said Prince Charles read books instead of spending time with her, and the two rarely had a moment alone on the yacht. She spoke of her exhaustion, her out-of-control bulimia, and her jealousy of Parker Bowles.

However, her friends painted a much different picture of the weeks after the wedding. Diana's butler, Paul Burrell, recalled a letter Diana wrote to a close friend about her time aboard *Britannia*:

> *I couldn't be happier. . . . Marriage suits me enormously. . . . It's the best thing that has ever happened to me—besides being the luckiest lady in the world.*[8]

After returning from their honeymoon in August, the couple invited the press to photograph them at Balmoral. The prince and princess seemed at ease with one another. The two held hands, and Diana rested her head on her husband's shoulder as the media clicked cameras and shouted questions.

"When [Diana] came back from the honeymoon . . . the expression on her face seemed to say, 'Phew, thank goodness.' She looked really relaxed that day, as if all the pressure had suddenly gone and she was taking a deep breath."[9]

—*Jayne Fincher, royal photographer*

▲ THE NEWLYWEDS PRESENTED THEMSELVES TO THE PRESS AT BALMORAL.

HER ROYAL HIGHNESS

Once the honeymoon was over, Diana faced a whole new set of challenges. She was not only

Prince Charles's wife, but also the Princess of Wales. People suddenly began treating Diana differently. It was not just that they now curtsied and addressed her as Your Royal Highness. Diana felt a distance opening between her and nonroyals—even close friends—that made her uncomfortable. The new princess also began receiving formal requests to help various charities. She knew she would need to overcome her nerves and self-doubt in order to fulfill her duties. On top of all this, she had to try to blend in with the rest of the royal family.

Diana was collapsing under the pressure. Bulimia wreaked havoc on her body. People were beginning to express concern about how unhealthy she looked, and her mind was equally unhealthy. Her illness, in combination with her jealous speculations about Parker Bowles, caused abrupt mood swings. The royal family's reaction only made things worse. Instead of sympathizing with Diana, they grew frustrated with her.

Prince Charles was the only one who came to Diana's aid. He sought professional help for his wife, but Diana was a difficult patient.

"One minute I was nobody, and the next minute I was Princess of Wales, mother, media toy, member of this family, and it was just too much for one person to handle."[10]

—*Diana*

In October 1981, the couple found out that another condition may have worsened Diana's mood swings and nausea. The Princess of Wales was pregnant.

————•◆•————

5

MOTHERHOOD

*D*iana was thrilled at the news of her pregnancy. Charles and Diana had little time to let the excitement sink in before they were whisked off on a three-day tour of Wales. During the tour, Diana had to face huge crowds, the press, and her fear of public speaking. All the while, she suffered from severe all-day morning sickness. Diana did her best to act calm and self-assured. She won over both people and press with her smile.

On the last day of the tour, Diana was exhausted, nauseous, and more nervous than

▶ DIANA CONTINUED TO MAKE PUBLIC APPEARANCES THROUGHOUT HER PREGNANCY.

ever. It was pouring rain as the royal couple's limo approached Caernarfon Castle, where Diana was scheduled to give her first speech. As they pulled up to the entrance, the princess lost all composure. Prince Charles gently reminded her of what her new position meant: "You've got to pull yourself together and do it."[1]

The prince escorted the reluctant princess to the podium. Diana stood uncertainly before the Welsh people for a few moments. Then she began her speech. Her attempt to express her thanks in Welsh was so well received that her audience gave her a standing ovation. The princess relaxed into the warmth of their approval and finished her speech with grace.

Afterwards, the Prince and Princess of Wales mingled with the crowds of people. Once she was among her people instead of in front of them, Diana felt in her element. She crouched down to greet children and accept their flowers and kisses. She warmed the hands of the elderly in her own. Prince Charles was proud and slightly in awe of his wife. Still, he felt a little hurt that his people seemed to love their princess more than their prince.

THE HEIR

On November 5, 1981, the royal family announced to the public that Diana was pregnant. The prince and princess were showered with gifts and good wishes. The royal family hoped Diana's happiness would last. But Diana's pregnancy was extremely difficult. She was sick nearly all the time and could barely sleep or eat. Yet she was still expected to carry out her duties as princess. When illness caused her to cancel public engagements or excuse herself from dinner, the queen was annoyed. Diana tried hard to hide her personal struggles and live up to the royal family's expectations, but it was especially difficult to hide from the persistent curiosity of the press.

On June 21, 1982, Diana gave birth to Prince William. Prince Charles was obviously delighted with his newborn son, and so was the rest of the country. For Diana, the first days of motherhood were blissful. But after she returned home from the hospital,

Diana's Cries for Help

Diana told her biographer she made several suicide attempts during the early years of her marriage. She recalled slicing open her chest and thighs with Prince Charles's penknife and trying to slit her wrists. When she was pregnant with Prince William, she reportedly threw herself down a flight of stairs to get her husband's attention. She said, "I was just so desperate. I knew what was wrong with me. . . . I just needed time to adapt to my new position."[2]

▲ DIANA AND CHARLES LEFT THE HOSPITAL WITH BABY WILLIAM ON JUNE 22, 1982.

darkness once again settled over the young princess.

Still battling bulimia, Diana also claimed to suffer from postpartum depression. Her mood swings and suspicions that her husband was cheating returned. The media picked up on Diana's problems and sketched unflattering caricatures of her in the news even as she sought treatment.

Whatever his relationship with Parker Bowles might have been, Charles remained supportive of Diana throughout this challenging period. The young family took up residence at their country home of Highgrove, where Charles and Diana experienced the ups and downs of their first several months of parenthood together.

DI-MANIA

By the spring of 1983, Diana seemed to have turned a fresh page in her life. She was 21 years old, gaining confidence as a wife and mother, and ready to tackle the role of princess. There was something about Diana as a new mother that particularly captured the hearts of the British people.

All eyes were on Charles, Diana, and William as the family set out on a tour of Australia and New Zealand in March. It was on this trip that Diana proved she was a new brand of royalty. She was going to do things differently. Any other royal mother would have left her child in the care of nannies, but Diana took William with her without asking the queen's permission. The unexpected move caused a sensation.

Diana's personality was charming, and she was much more approachable than other royals. The princess laughed easily and had a clever sense of humor. Everyone, especially children, felt comfortable and cared for in her presence. "There was more depth and warmth in her concern for us than any words can describe," said a local fire chief in Canberra, Australia.[3] The Australian people adored Princess Diana so much that if Prince Charles approached them instead, they groaned. If the prince was jealous of his wife's popularity, he did not show it. The royal couple seemed comfortable and content. As the press broadcast glamorous images of the happy family, the world fell in love.

A SECOND SON

By February 1984, Diana was pregnant again. During Prince Charles's frequent absences between the births of William and Harry, Diana sometimes wondered if he had rekindled his relationship with Parker Bowles. Still, Diana later remembered the final weeks of her second pregnancy as a time when she and her husband were closer than they had ever been.

The birth of Prince Harry on September 15, 1984, was cause for national celebration. Heaps of baby clothes arrived in the mail, sent with love by the adoring public. By some accounts, both Charles and Diana had wished for a girl, but their delight with both boys was obvious.

The prince and princess enjoyed being parents. Both were actively involved in caring for their children. The prince neglected his royal duties to spend more time with his family. Diana was a national symbol of devoted motherhood. Prince William adored his baby brother, covering him "in an endless supply of hugs and kisses."[4] It seemed nothing could destroy the happiness of this young royal family.

Succession to the Throne

Princes William and Harry were born second and third in line for the British throne. Prince Charles would become king after his mother's reign ended, and Prince William would someday take the place of his father. When William and Harry were born, the order of succession was determined by gender and birth order. The eldest son of the monarch was first in line, followed by the monarch's younger sons. After the youngest son came the eldest daughter, and then the younger daughters in order of birth. Additionally, no one who was a Roman Catholic or married one could succeed to the throne. Elizabeth II became queen because her father had no sons and no brothers who were eligible for the throne.

These laws changed in 2011 so that sons would not be preferred over daughters. In the future, beginning with the children of Prince William, succession will be determined solely by birth order. Whether male or female, the monarch's eldest child will be first in line for the throne. The heir to the throne will also be able to marry a Roman Catholic if he or she chooses.

6

THE PEOPLE'S PRINCESS

After Harry's birth in 1984, rumors of trouble in Charles and Diana's marriage took root. Many believed Charles, having produced the obligatory "heir and a spare" with Diana, felt free to return to his former love, Parker Bowles. Surely these rumors fueled Diana's suspicions she had never been the only woman in her husband's life. The press also speculated that Diana and Charles had little in common, she was trying to change him and chase away those close to him, and she spent too much of his money.

▶ AFTER HARRY'S BIRTH, DIANA BEGAN FOCUSING HER ENERGY ON HER CHARITABLE WORK.

Though the Prince and Princess of Wales denied the vicious rumors, they seemed to be drifting apart. Diana began pursuing her own interests more aggressively at the end of 1984. She became involved in charities that supported young children, people with disabilities, and the elderly. Everyone was impressed with the way she handled herself and the effort she put into her work.

In addition to Diana's growing independence in the public sphere, the princess was firm about how she wanted to raise her

Fashion Icon

Although Diana viewed helping people as the most important aspect of her role as princess, others were often more interested in what she wore. From the moment she appeared on the steps of Saint Paul's Cathedral in her frothy wedding gown, Diana became a fashion icon. The editor of *Vogue* helped Diana develop her everyday style. Diana soon took to wearing elegant suits and modest dresses. She chose garments with high necklines and had weights sewn into the hems of her skirts so the wind could not budge them. Palace protocol required several changes of clothes throughout the day. In the evenings, Diana clothed her tall, thin frame in dazzling gowns. Her clothing choices reflected her transition from an unsure teenager to a glamorous woman, and later into a businesslike humanitarian. Women wanted to be like her, dress like her, and even wear the same hairstyle. The British fashion industry took off. "Year by year, [Diana] became more sophisticated and more sure of herself," said fashion designer Valentino. "Every designer was inspired by her. To me, she will remain one of the most beautiful . . . ladies in the world."[1]

▲ DIANA AND CHARLES DROPPED OFF WILLIAM FOR HIS
FIRST DAY OF KINDERGARTEN ON SEPTEMBER 24, 1985.

children. She wanted them to go to school with
other children, learn to do things for themselves,
and have at least some of the freedoms of other
boys their age. This more informal way of raising
her boys brought Diana even closer to the British
people. The royal family—including Prince
Charles—disapproved of the break with tradition,
but they did not stop her.

DISTANT TRAVELERS

In April 1985, Charles and Diana—who were
known as the Waleses—spent 17 days in Italy.
Their partnership seemed strong, though many

suspected they were just keeping up appearances. In October, they arrived in Australia. The Australians made it clear Diana was the one they wanted to see, not Charles. This time, Prince Charles seemed to take the treatment more personally.

The couple arrived in the United States in November. In Washington DC, Diana visited a hospice facility before appearing at the White House for dinner and dancing. Once again, Diana stole the show in an off-the-shoulder gown. Prince Charles got his chance to shine during a polo match in Florida, but he still felt underappreciated.

COLLAPSE

The prince and princess arrived home just in time for Charles's thirty-seventh birthday. A large celebration was to be held in December at the Royal Opera House. Unbeknownst to her husband, Diana had something special planned for him. Toward the end of the evening of skits and other lighthearted entertainment, Diana excused herself from the royal box. Everyone was shocked when she appeared onstage a few minutes later in a gown of slinky satin. The first notes of Billy Joel's "Uptown Girl" sounded, and Diana performed a dance routine she had been working on with dance partner Wayne Sleep. Diana's performance was honored with a standing ovation. But all she really wanted was her husband's approval.

Prince Charles did not see his wife's performance as a gesture of affection. He saw it as an embarrassment to the royal family. He also felt it as a personal slight. Diana made herself the center of attention once again before his wounded pride had healed. Prince Charles could not completely hide his annoyance, and his coolness toward Diana did not go unnoticed.

Around this time, Sarah "Fergie" Ferguson was developing a serious relationship with Prince Andrew, Charles's younger brother. Diana appeared especially unhappy and frail next to the sturdy, spunky Ferguson. And the passion between Ferguson and Prince Andrew was a stark contrast to the distance between Diana and Prince Charles. On a ski trip in January 1986, Charles reportedly asked Diana, "Why can't you be more like

The Wild Wives

Ferguson and Diana first met at a polo match while Diana was dating Prince Charles and soon became close friends. The public naturally began to draw comparisons between the two women. Diana felt pressure to imitate the fun-loving Ferguson, and she began to tag along on the redhead's wild escapades. The two women crashed parties, dressed up in silly costumes, and poked people's bottoms with umbrellas. These antics only hurt their reputations.

▲ DIANA AND SARAH FERGUSON ENJOYED EACH OTHER'S COMPANY.

Fergie?"[2] Ferguson and Prince Andrew married on July 23, 1986.

That spring, the Prince and Princess of Wales toured Canada and Japan together. With her marriage collapsing, Diana was again in the throes of bulimia. She was so weak and exhausted that she fainted during a public engagement in Vancouver, Canada. She got no sympathy from her husband, who felt she should have found a way to keep her ill health private.

"IRRETRIEVABLY BROKEN DOWN"

It was in 1986 that the Waleses' marriage became fractured beyond repair. Prince Charles dubbed it "irretrievably broken down."[3] His relationship with Parker Bowles, he later admitted, had crossed the line between friendship and romance.

Charles and Diana began spending more and more of their private time apart. In public, however, they still showed a united front.

Soon after the royal couple returned from their spring tour abroad, Diana got to know Captain James Hewitt, who was in charge of the stables at Buckingham Palace. This appealed to Diana because she had been looking for someone to help her overcome her fear of riding.

During the riding lessons, the two became close friends. Diana was relieved to finally have someone in whom she could confide her daily struggles. Hewitt was aware of her disintegrating marriage, and he gave Diana sympathy. Over time, their friendship progressed into an affair.

SEPARATE LIVES

In 1987, the press began tracking the days the Prince and Princess of Wales spent apart. The public was appalled at reports that Prince Charles had spent more than a month at Balmoral without his wife and children. Palace staff gossiped that even when the two were together, they slept in separate bedrooms. Charles and Diana continued their affairs in secrecy, coming together for the sake of their sons and the monarchy.

▲ THIS PHOTO PUBLICIZED DIANA'S WORK WITH AIDS
PATIENTS AND HELPED LESSEN PUBLIC FEAR OF THE
ILLNESS.

Charles relaxed with Parker Bowles, pursued
his own interests, and championed his own
causes, including the arts, education, and
environmental sustainability. Meanwhile, Diana
had plenty of time to devote to charity work.
In April 1987, she was invited to Middlesex
Hospital for the opening of the first acquired
immunodeficiency syndrome (AIDS) ward in
the United Kingdom. At the time, many people
believed they could contract AIDS simply by
touching someone who had it. Diana knew

better. A photograph of the princess shaking hands with an AIDS patient made headlines worldwide. That moment solidified the world's view of Diana as much more than a wife, mother, and fashion icon.

THE END OF SHY DI

Diana became more comfortable in her independent role throughout 1988. As a testament to her growing self-assurance, Diana sought treatment for bulimia during this period. Despite the length of Diana's struggle with the disorder, her doctor gave her an optimistic prognosis. "He helped me get back my self-esteem," Diana later said.[4] With newfound physical and mental health, Diana was able to throw herself completely into her work. She was growing adept at using her star status to get people interested in humanitarian issues that were important to her.

Erasing Taboos

At the time Diana began her AIDS awareness campaign, the disease carried a stubborn stigma. Many believed AIDS was as contagious as the common cold and were afraid to even go near a person suffering from the disease. With a single gesture, Diana cut through these prejudices. "Here was the world's most famous woman embracing AIDS with one simple act . . . and with that handshake, she educated the world about compassion, love, and understanding," said David Harvey, founder of the AIDS Alliance for Children, Youth, and Families.[5] Diana would continue to educate the public about the human immunodeficiency virus (HIV) and AIDS throughout the rest of her life.

7

THE WAR OF THE WALESES

By the end of 1989, Diana's relationship with Hewitt had fizzled. He planned to go abroad with his regiment, and the princess could not convince him to stay. In his absence, Diana sought the companionship of James Gilbey, a friend from her single days. The two had a flirtatious telephone conversation on New Year's Eve, in which Gilbey affectionately called Diana "Squidgy." Royal phone conversations were routinely recorded, but they were supposed to remain private, and Diana could not have guessed

▶ AS THEIR CHILDREN GREW UP, DIANA AND CHARLES GREW FURTHER APART.

at the time what trouble the phone call would later cause.

The emotional distance between Diana and Charles became uncomfortably apparent in June 1990. Prince Charles fell off his horse and broke his arm during a polo match. The injury required two operations, and Diana showed unusual tenderness toward her husband after he came home from the hospital. However, Prince Charles said he would rather be alone. Diana felt rejected. She was further humiliated by the fact that Charles was more than happy to let Parker Bowles take care of him in private.

ALONE AND DISAPPOINTED

Going into 1991, Diana felt trapped and alone. She somehow needed her voice to be heard. That spring, Diana began working with journalist Andrew Morton on her biography.

The public did catch a glimpse of what life was like for the princess in June 1991. Diana received word that Prince William had been

Telling Her Story

Diana cooperated with Morton on her biography, but she never met him. To keep their interaction secret, he sent her interview questions by mail. Diana recorded her answers on tape and sent them back. Morton also reached out to Diana's friends to get a more accurate picture of her life. The fact that Diana and Morton were never seen together later helped her argue that she had nothing to do with what he wrote.

seriously injured while at school. Another boy had accidentally hit the young prince in the head with a golf club. William's skull was fractured, and there was a small risk of brain damage. It was the month of the prince's ninth birthday.

Diana met Prince Charles at the hospital, where a computerized axial tomography (CAT) scan revealed that with surgery, a full recovery was likely for William. Diana was there to comfort her son before and after the surgery. Prince Charles, satisfied that his son's life was not in danger, had already left on an official engagement. Although the surgery went well, Diana was disappointed that her husband would put duty before family in such a situation. And when the news of Charles's behavior spread, the country was shocked. One newspaper headline accusingly asked of Charles, "What Kind of Dad Are You?"[1]

The partnership between the Prince and Princess of Wales continued to unravel throughout the rest of 1991. Diana celebrated her thirtieth birthday without her husband. Those on Charles's side were quick to defend him, saying he offered to throw her a party and she refused. The two celebrated their tenth anniversary in privacy while rumors swirled around them.

A TERRIBLE YEAR

The next year, 1992, was a difficult year for the entire royal family. January brought evidence that Prince Andrew's marriage to Ferguson was crumbling. The couple announced their formal separation in March. That same month, Diana's father fell seriously ill. Prince Charles had hoped to redeem his image by taking the family to a ski resort in Austria. However, Diana wanted to be at her father's side. She was also concerned about William's head injury the year before. By the time the family was scheduled to leave for Austria, Diana's father was almost fully recovered. Doctors promised he would soon be discharged. They also convinced Diana that William was well enough to try skiing. The Waleses decided to go on the trip after all.

On March 29, Diana received the news that her father had died of a heart attack that day. The family had just recently arrived in Austria, but the princess wanted to return to London to attend his funeral alone. Ultimately, though, the pressure to appear as a family prevailed. Prince Charles accompanied his wife on the flight to London. The two traveled separately to the funeral.

As Diana grieved for her father, Queen Elizabeth grieved for the monarchy. In April,

▲ DIANA, SHOWN HERE IN 1991, WAS A FREQUENT VISITOR TO AUSTRIAN SKI RESORTS.

Princess Anne—the queen's daughter—divorced her husband. The queen knew Prince Charles's marriage had also reached a breaking point. The

Although the year marked the fortieth anniversary of her ascension to the throne, the queen called 1992 her "annus horribilis." That year, the deterioration of three of her four children's marriages were topped off by a fire at Windsor Castle. In her speech, the queen acknowledged the monarchy was not infallible. She asked her people to temper their criticism with "a touch of gentleness, good humor, and understanding."[2]

lives of the British royals had become the world's most fascinating soap opera.

THE BATTLE RAGES ON

June 1992 marked a turning point in the war of the Waleses. The publication of Morton's biography, *Diana: Her True Story*, shocked the world. Within its pages lay accusations that Prince Charles had broken Diana's spirit early in their marriage, had never ceased his relationship with Parker Bowles, and may never have loved his wife. The royal family was furious at this brutal assault on the reputation of the future king. Diana responded to their anger by denying any cooperation with Morton. Few were fooled.

In some ways, Diana got what she wanted as a result of the biography. The British people responded to the book with an outpouring of sympathy for her. Additionally, Prince Charles agreed to talk with her about the possibility of a separation. A separation was appealing because it would give Diana a certain amount of freedom without extinguishing hopes of reconciliation in

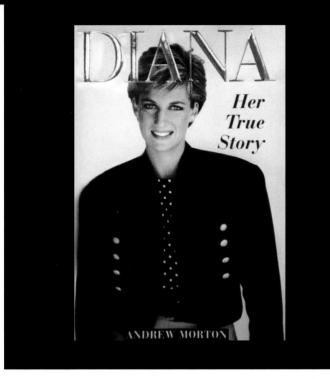

▲ DIANA'S BOOK WITH ANDREW MORTON TOLD THE
PRINCESS'S SIDE OF THE STORY.

the future. However, a separation would not be
possible without the queen's approval.

August brought more humiliation for the
royal family. Photographs of Ferguson with a
boyfriend were splashed across the pages of the
country's newspapers. That same month, to
Diana's horror, her taped phone conversation
with Gilbey was leaked to the press. This incident
was incriminating enough to cause a scandal.

The Prince and Princess of Wales dutifully
suffered through a joint tour of South Korea in

November, failing to hide their feelings. Prince Charles hired Jonathan Dimbleby to write his biography and conduct a television interview to tell his side of the story. By December, it was clear the charade of the Waleses could not continue. That month, the couple separated formally.

ROAD TO DIVORCE

Separation seemed ideal, but various pressures drove the couple toward a more permanent solution. The following year, 1993, began with the release of a recording of an intimate and racy telephone conversation between Prince Charles and Parker Bowles. Diana was sickened by the recording. So were the royal family and the public. For the time being, Diana emerged as the triumphant victor in the battle for the public's support.

The prince's television interview with Dimbleby aired in June 1994. Officially, it was a celebration of Charles's twenty-fifth year as Prince of Wales. Unofficially, it was an opportunity for Prince Charles to redeem himself in the eyes of the public. The prince admitted to having an affair with Parker Bowles, though he claimed the affair had begun only after his marriage to Diana had failed. Dimbleby's *The Prince of Wales: A Biography* was published in the fall. The reaction was mixed. Many admired Prince Charles's openness; others were appalled at his confession of infidelity. Diana later recalled her reaction to the interview: "My first concern was for the children. I wanted to protect them. I was pretty devastated myself. But then I admired the honesty."[3]

Diana wanted to have the last word in this public battle. In November 1995, she arranged to sit for a secret interview with Martin Bashir for the BBC network's current affairs program *Panorama*. When the interview aired on November 20, just days after Prince Charles's forty-seventh birthday, millions of viewers

Royal Marriage Counselors

Queen Elizabeth and her husband, Prince Philip, understood Diana and Charles's difficulties perhaps better than anyone. Their marriage had felt the strain of decades of pressure and scrutiny. From the beginning, Prince Philip had struggled to accept the fact that his wife would not take his name. "I am nothing but a bloody amoeba," he reportedly complained. "I am the only man in the country not allowed to give his name to his own children."[4] Queen Elizabeth would always hold the power in their relationship, yet the royal couple found ways to get past this imbalance and keep their marriage strong.

The queen and her husband hoped Diana and Charles would also be able to sort out their differences in time. The queen would not agree to a separation until Charles and Diana had at least made an effort to save their marriage. Throughout the summer of 1992, the queen and her husband tried their best to be impartial advisors. Ultimately, though, their loyalty lay with their son.

▲ DIANA SPOKE ABOUT MANY PRIVATE THINGS DURING HER INTERVIEW ON *PANORAMA.*

were struck by Diana's sincerity. She spoke from her heart about her marriage, her eating disorder, the royal family, and her vision of the future. The princess confessed to an affair with James Hewitt, but her audience thought it seemed justified considering her husband's longstanding relationship with Parker Bowles.

Perhaps the most controversial subject Diana addressed was the future of the monarchy. She acknowledged the need for a closer relationship between the monarchy and the public, implied Prince Charles would not adapt well to being king, and confessed she did not believe she would become queen but rather "a queen of people's hearts."[5] Diana wanted to assume the role of ambassador and nurturer for her country.

Although her famous *Panorama* interview endeared her to the public, it also drew the wrath of Buckingham Palace. The royal family could no longer endure the public outbursts of their son and daughter-in-law. By the close of 1995, the queen was convinced divorce was the only reasonable course of action. She asked Charles and Diana to begin negotiations. Diana officially agreed to the divorce, and the press announced her decision February 29, 1996.

The divorce was finalized on August 28, 1996. Diana was allowed to stay at Kensington Palace and given £17 million, which was approximately $26 million at the time. However, she was stripped of the title Her Royal Highness. From then on she would be simply Diana, Princess of Wales. Diana would never become queen, though her sons would remain Charles's heirs.

———•◆•———

8

QUEEN OF PEOPLE'S HEARTS

With Diana's divorce from Charles came sadness and another reinvention of her role in public life. But the divorce also gave Diana a new level of freedom. She no longer needed the approval of the royal family to live the way she wanted. During the summer of 1996, Diana began centering her focus. She wrote to approximately 100 charities and politely withdrew her support. The princess wanted to devote her full attention to the causes that were most important to her: AIDS, cancer, leprosy,

▶ DIANA ATTENDED MANY BENEFITS IN SUPPORT OF HER FAVORITE CAUSES.

After her divorce, Diana dated Dr. Hasnat Kahn, whom she had met in 1995. He was a kind man and as devoted to helping others as Diana was. The two dated seriously for a while after her divorce. However, both Diana and Kahn put their work before their relationship, and they broke up in late spring of 1997.

homeless youth, sick and disabled children, and ballet. Diana was also looking forward to her upcoming tour with the Red Cross to raise awareness about land mines.

ANGEL IN ANGOLA

In mid-January 1997, Diana arrived in Angola. This war-torn country in southwestern Africa had been devastated by land mines. Angola's people—many of them missing limbs—seemed in desperate need of whatever love and attention the princess could give.

Diana was particularly drawn to a little girl she met in a tiny village hospital. Seven-year-old Helen had accidentally stepped on a mine on her way to fetch water for her family. The princess calmly stood by as a nurse pulled down a sheet to reveal the girl's horrific wound. The mine had blown open the girl's stomach. Diana looked into Helen's eyes and gently took her hand. After a few moments, Diana pulled the sheet back up to cover the girl's wound. After Diana had gone, Helen reportedly asked, "Is [Diana] an angel?"[1]

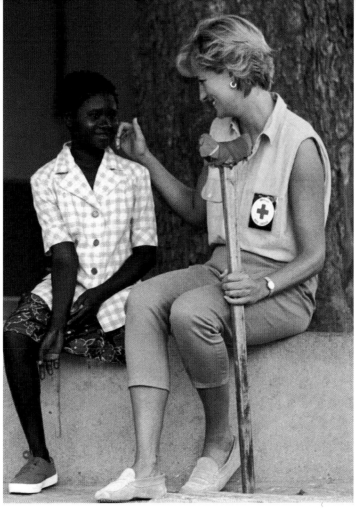

▲ DIANA TALKED WITH A LAND MINE VICTIM IN ANGOLA IN 1997.

Hours after receiving comfort from the princess, the little girl passed away.

Later, Diana traveled to Kuito, one of the towns most affected by land mines. Images of the princess walking on a path through a minefield proved her sincerity to the world. The body armor and helmet she wore were indications of the great risk she was taking to support this cause. Diana did away with accusations that her trip was about politics or public relations when she simply stated, "I am a humanitarian. I always have been and I always will be."[2]

The princess proved the truth of this statement time and again by comforting Angola's wounded. Photographs of Diana spending time with land mine survivors—especially children—earned the cause worldwide attention. In the spring of 1997, Diana followed up her Angola tour by pushing for a land mine ban in the United Kingdom and the United States. She also planned a trip to Bosnia in August.

THE LAST SUMMER

Earlier that year, Diana had decided to auction off several of her dresses and give the proceeds to AIDS and cancer charities. The auction had been William's idea. Musician Elton John, with whom the princess had become close friends, encouraged it. The auction became a reality on June 25, 1997, in New York City. It was a huge success. Diana was able to raise more than $3 million in a single evening.

In July, Mohamed al-Fayed, the owner of the luxury department store Harrods, invited Diana and her sons to spend time with him and his family in France in July. Al-Fayed was a friend of the Spencer family. He was a controversial figure, but he also provided Diana with an escape at the perfect time. Parker Bowles had received increased media attention after divorcing her husband in 1995. A television documentary about her was scheduled to air that month. Prince Charles had also announced he was throwing a party for her fiftieth birthday at Highgrove on July 18. It

The al-Fayeds

Mohamed al-Fayed was born in Egypt in 1933. He founded a business there and amassed a fortune before moving to the United Kingdom in the 1960s. Though his application to become a British citizen was denied, his billionaire status gave him a certain amount of influence. He reportedly used it to help bring the Labour Party to prominence, ruining the reputations of a few Conservative politicians along the way. In 1985, al-Fayed bought House of Fraser, a department store group that included Harrods and more than 60 other stores. Harrods is a luxury department store that was founded in 1849, and al-Fayed spent more than £400 million, or approximately $420 million at the time, to restore it to its former glory.

Dodi, al-Fayed's son, was born Emad Mohamed al-Fayed in 1955. He was a film producer, and his portfolio included films such as *Chariots of Fire* (1981), *Hook* (1991), and *The Scarlet Letter* (1995). He had a reputation for being primarily a pleasure-seeker.

▲ DIANA AND DODI AL-FAYED WERE TOGETHER IN SAINT
TROPEZ, FRANCE, IN AUGUST 1997.

was as good as announcing they were officially
together.

The princess knew people would be clamoring
to see her reaction to the interest in Parker
Bowles. Rather than give them the pleasure,
she decided to join the al-Fayeds with her boys.
In a typical display of extravagance, al-Fayed
had purchased a yacht, the *Jonikal*, for the
occasion. He also invited his son Dodi along

to amuse Diana. The water, sun, and luxurious surroundings seemed to refresh everyone. A spark of romance was also in the air. Diana and Dodi were growing closer.

On July 20, Diana departed for London with her boys. When the princess returned to the *Jonikal* and the younger al-Fayed's company at the end of July, she left William and Harry behind. As the couple sailed along the coast of Sardinia, they picked up their relationship where they had left off. Photographers captured images of the two kissing and holding hands.

Diana and al-Fayed returned to London in early August. The two kept in touch while Diana campaigned against land mines in Bosnia. There, she brought joy to victims who vividly remembered the date their world literally exploded. "My accident was on July 29, 1981," she joked, referring to her wedding to Prince Charles.[3] Later, the princess saw a woman laying flowers on her son's grave. Diana gathered the woman into her arms and touched her face. Diana was transcending her role as a British princess to become an international humanitarian.

9

A Candle in the Wind

*D*iana was reunited with al-Fayed once again in late August. The couple enjoyed another private cruise on the *Jonikal*, though it was difficult to avoid the press. Many believed Diana and al-Fayed were headed toward marriage. Whatever the case, those late summer days on the ocean were blissful. The pair planned to end their trip in Paris, France. Diana would then fly back to London, where she was looking forward to seeing William and Harry.

▲ WITH A NEW LOVE AND IMPORTANT CHARITY WORK, DIANA'S LIFE WAS LOOKING UP IN THE SUMMER OF 1997.

AUGUST 30–31, 1997

Diana and al-Fayed arrived in Paris on Saturday, August 30, and checked into the Ritz Hotel. The paparazzi were waiting for them. Diana had her hair done at the hotel while al-Fayed visited a nearby jewelry store, fueling rumors that he intended to propose to her. Then the couple retired to al-Fayed's apartment for a couple of hours before dinner. As the press had also caught wind of their dinner plans, Diana and al-Fayed decided to switch restaurants at the last minute.

The couple returned to the Ritz to eat. Even there, the paparazzi were relentless. The famous couple escaped to the hotel's Imperial Suite to dine in peace and plot the best route back to al-Fayed's apartment, where they were planning to spend the night. Al-Fayed came up with a plan.

The couple's driver would leave from the hotel's front entrance in the vehicle they arrived in. This decoy would distract the press while Diana and al-Fayed made their exit from the hotel's rear entrance. The couple left the Ritz at 12:20 a.m. in a black Mercedes. Henri Paul, a trusted employee of al-Fayed, was the driver. Bodyguard Trevor Rees-Jones also accompanied them.

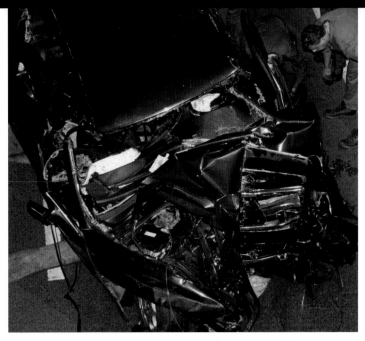

▲ THE FORCE OF THE CRASH CRUMPLED THE CAR
CONTAINING DIANA, AL-FAYED, PAUL, AND REES-JONES.

As Paul sped away from the Ritz, Diana and
al-Fayed turned to look out the rear window
at the small group of paparazzi chasing them.
Minutes later, after running a red light, the
Mercedes zoomed into a tunnel. Photographers
were still hot on the trail. Paul attempted to
veer around a slower vehicle. He was too close.
The cars brushed against each other. Suddenly,
Paul lost control of the vehicle. The car careened
head-on into a concrete pillar, crumpling the
hood. For those inside the car, everything went
black.

HELP ARRIVES

People who happened to be driving through the tunnel at the time remember hearing a horrific sound that might have been an explosion. Photographers and passersby were drawn like magnets to the mangled Mercedes. Frederic Maillez, an off-duty doctor, administered first aid to Diana as cameras flashed around him. Others tended to Rees-Jones, who was conscious but had multiple injuries. Paul and al-Fayed were killed on impact.

Slumped on the floor in front of the backseat, Diana was still breathing and appeared to be the least injured of the four. Maillez had no way of knowing the force of the collision tore Diana's heart from its place in her chest and threw it to the other side of her body.

Ambulances arrived within minutes of the crash. The rescue team worked carefully to free Diana from the wrecked car. Before she could be loaded into the ambulance, they tried to stabilize her. However, Diana suffered a heart attack at the scene. It was clear now that Diana's internal injuries were life threatening. Finally, with Diana on a respirator and her heart weak but beating, the princess was taken to the nearest hospital.

Diana arrived at the hospital just after 2:00 a.m. Doctors found severe internal injuries. Her pulmonary vein and the sac around her heart were torn and bleeding heavily. Then the princess suffered a second heart attack. Surgeons worked for two hours, but they could not revive her, and the princess was pronounced dead at 4:00 a.m. Diana's family was notified. They began making arrangements to transport her body home.

A WORLD IN MOURNING

When the news broke to the public later that morning, shock and confusion reigned. How could this have been allowed to happen? Some people were quick to blame the paparazzi or suspect an assassination plot. However, an autopsy on Paul revealed the driver's blood alcohol content was three times the

Conspiracy Theories

After the crash, many thought Diana had been assassinated. Mohamed al-Fayed claimed Diana and his son had planned to marry, and even that the princess had been pregnant with his son's child. He believed Diana's intention to start a family with a Muslim man would have been enough reason for her to be targeted. Diana also reportedly predicted someone would try to kill her.

There are many theories about how the alleged assassination could have been carried out. Some claim the British Secret Intelligence Service orchestrated the accident, arranging the evidence to make it look like the driver was at fault. Others believe the Mercedes had been tampered with so Paul was sure to lose control. Or perhaps the driver of the other car involved in the crash was hired to cause the accident. Investigation into these theories revealed none of the claims held true. Diana's death was a tragic accident.

legal limit at the time of the crash. There were also traces of prescription drugs in his system. Investigators later concluded Paul's impaired driving was responsible for Diana's death.

As the loss sank in, people brought their grief to the gates of Kensington Palace. Bouquets of flowers, notes to the princess, and personal mementos piled around the princess's former home. At night, mourners were illuminated by the soft glow of candles. Meanwhile, the royal family grieved at Balmoral. Their distance angered the British people. They felt abandoned and longed for words of comfort from their queen.

The day before the funeral, the royal family returned to London. Prince Charles guided William and Harry through the tributes to their mother at Kensington Palace. The boys bravely accepted the condolences of the public. The queen honored the profound atmosphere of grief by lowering the Union Flag, the United Kingdom's flag, atop Buckingham Palace to half-mast for the first time in history.

That evening, the queen spoke to her people. She described Diana as "an exceptional and gifted human being" and one who "never lost her capacity . . . to inspire others with her warmth and kindness."[1] The queen expressed her hope that Diana's funeral the following day would be an opportunity for the nation to come together in both grief and gratitude. The nation generally accepted their queen's tribute as a warm and sincere voice to their grief. They were glad their queen was showing love and respect toward their princess.

SAYING FAREWELL

Saturday, September 6, 1997, dawned in London with mourners already crowding the streets. They were reverently quiet as the funeral procession passed by on its way to Westminster Abbey. Diana's coffin was mounted

The Princes Grow Up

After Diana's death, William and Harry grew up much in the way their mother would have wanted. The boys attended school with other upper-class children their age. Though William especially was raised to honor duty and tradition because he was the heir, the boys had plenty of fun growing up. They played sports, dated whomever they chose regardless of class, and even indulged in some activities that might have been viewed as unbefitting of princes. Although images of the princes behaving irresponsibly have been published in the tabloids, both William and Harry take their duties seriously. They have both followed in their mother's footsteps, offering their services to help disadvantaged people around the world. Both boys also served in the British Army. Though Diana's absence from their lives is far from forgotten, the princes welcomed Parker Bowles, their stepmother, into the family in 2005. Catherine Middleton also joined the royal family in 2011 as Prince William's wife.

on a gun carriage pulled by horses and surrounded by guards. It was draped in the Royal Standard—the flag of the monarchy. On top of the flag lay bouquets of white lilies, tulips, and roses. Nestled in the rose bouquet was a sealed envelope that read "Mum." It was a card from Prince Harry. Only the tolling of bells and the sound of hooves striking pavement broke the silence.

As the procession came to Buckingham Palace, all eyes were on the royal family. The queen bowed to Diana's coffin as it passed in a gesture of solemn respect. Other members of the royal family followed suit. At Saint James's Palace, Princes Charles, Philip, William, and Harry joined the procession. They walked to the church behind Diana's coffin along with Diana's brother, Charles Spencer.

The guards carried the princess's coffin into Westminster Abbey for the funeral service. Then the church filled with music. First the national anthem played, followed by Verdi's *Requiem*. Elton John's version of "Candle in the Wind" was a memorable addition to the event. Diana's sisters gave readings, as did Prime Minister Tony Blair. Spencer's speech was another heartfelt tribute to "the unique, the complex, the extraordinary and irreplaceable Diana."[2] The end of the funeral mass

▲ WELL WISHERS LEFT TRIBUTES OUTSIDE SAINT JAMES'S CHAPEL IN LONDON IN THE DAYS BEFORE DIANA'S FUNERAL.

was marked by a minute of silence. Then the bells rang out as Diana's coffin was carried from the church. As the hearse drove Diana to her final resting place, the crowds broke into applause—a final show of affection for their Princess of Wales.

Diana lives on in the memories of the millions of people whose lives she touched. She dismantled prejudices, and she brought awareness around AIDS, land mines, eating disorders, and so many other issues. The world will never forget her lessons in love, compassion, and understanding. And Diana, Princess of Wales will forever be a queen of people's hearts.

TIMELINE

1961

Diana Frances Spencer is born on July 1.

1969

Diana's parents divorce.

1975

Diana's father becomes the eighth Earl of Spencer, and she becomes Lady Diana.

1980

Diana begins dating Prince Charles in July.

1981

The wedding of Prince Charles to Lady Diana takes place on July 29.

1982

Prince William is born on June 21.

1977

Diana first meets Prince Charles at Althorp in November. She is 16 years old.

1978

Diana drops out of school in Switzerland and returns to London to find work.

1979

Diana is hired as a kindergarten teacher.

1983

Princess Diana and Prince Charles bring their son along on a tour of Australia and New Zealand in March.

1984

Prince Harry is born on September 15.

1986

Prince Charles resumes his romance with Camilla Parker Bowles. Diana begins an affair with Captain James Hewitt.

TIMELINE

1987

Diana shakes hands with an AIDS patient at Middlesex Hospital in April. The photograph makes headlines around the world.

1989

Diana's conversation with James Gilbey is recorded on December 31. It is later released and causes a scandal.

1992

Andrew Morton's *Diana: Her True Story* is published in June.

1996

The divorce of the Prince and Princess of Wales is finalized on August 28.

1997

Diana begins her campaign to ban land mines with a tour of Angola in January.

1997

Diana auctions off several of her dresses in New York on June 25. She raises more than $3 million for her charities.

1992

Princess Diana and Prince Charles formally separate in December.

1994

Author Jonathan Dimbleby helps Prince Charles repair his image following the publication of the Morton biography.

1995

Diana's *Panorama* interview for the BBC airs on November 20.

1997

Diana and her boys join the al-Fayeds on their yacht, the *Jonikal*, in July, and the princess begins a romance with Dodi al-Fayed.

1997

Diana dies in a violent car accident on August 31. Al-Fayed and Henri Paul, the driver, are also killed.

1997

Diana's funeral is held on September 6. The princess is honored as a member of the royal family.

QUICK FACTS

DATE OF BIRTH
July 1, 1961

PLACE OF BIRTH
Park House in Norfolk, England

DATE OF DEATH
August 31, 1997

PLACE OF DEATH
Paris, France

PARENTS
Johnnie and Frances Spencer

MARRIAGE
Charles, Prince of Wales (1981–1996)

CHILDREN
Prince William
Prince Harry

CAREER HIGHLIGHTS

Diana worked with a variety of charities throughout her life. She is remembered especially for her success in educating people about HIV/AIDS. She also devoted her efforts to victims of leprosy and cancer, survivors of land mines, and sick, disabled, and homeless youth. In the later years of her life, Diana focused her attention on a few charitable organizations she identified most closely with.

QUOTE

"One minute I was nobody, and the next minute I was Princess of Wales, mother, media toy, member of this family, and it was just too much for one person to handle."—*Diana*

 GLOSSARY

alienate
To lose affection or become estranged.

boarding school
A school where students live away from home.

bulimia
A serious eating disorder characterized by overeating and self-induced vomiting.

decoy
Something that draws attention away from something else.

governess
A woman who supervises or tutors a child in the home.

humanitarian
A person who works for social reform and improving peoples' lives.

land mine
A device planted in the ground that explodes when vehicles or people pass over it.

paparazzi
Aggressive photojournalists who take pictures of celebrities and sell them to media outlets.

postpartum depression
A mother's hormonal changes, fatigue, and psychological adjustment to motherhood in the period following birth leading to sadness or mental health problems.

prognosis
> The likelihood of recovery.

protocol
> A code of etiquette.

pulmonary vein
> A vein that returns oxygenated blood from the lungs to the heart.

regiment
> A unit of military troops.

succession
> The order in which a group of people inherit a title or property.

transcript
> A written copy of something that was spoken aloud.

ADDITIONAL RESOURCES

SELECTED BIBLIOGRAPHY

Bradford, Sarah. *Diana*. New York: Viking, 2006. Print.

Coward, Rosalind. *Diana: The Portrait*. Kansas City, MO: Andrews McMeel, 2007. Print.

Edwards, Anne. *Ever After: Diana and the Life She Led*. New York: St. Martin's, 1999. Print.

Morton, Andrew. *Diana: Her True Story—In Her Own Words*. New York: Simon, 1997. Print.

FURTHER READINGS

Andersen, Christopher P. *After Diana: William, Harry, Charles, and the Royal House of Windsor*. New York: Hyperion, 2007. Print.

Brown, Tina. *The Diana Chronicles*. New York: Doubleday, 2007. Print.

WEB LINKS

To learn more about Diana, visit ABDO Publishing Company online at **www.abdopublishing.com**. Web sites about Diana are featured on our Book Links page. These links are routinely monitored and updated to provide the most current information available.

FOR MORE INFORMATION

For more information on this subject, contact or visit the following organizations.

Althorp Estate

The Stables, Althorp, Northamptonshire NN7 4HQ, United Kingdom
+44 (0)16 0477 0107
www.althorp.com
Diana's former home is also her burial site. Her grave lies on an island in the middle of a lake called the Round Oval. Only family members are allowed to visit the island, but visitors can pay their respects at a lakeshore shrine to the princess.

Buckingham Palace

Buckingham Palace, London SW1A 1AA, United Kingdom
+44 (0)20 7766 7300
www.royalcollection.org.uk/visit/buckinghampalace
Visit the home of the British monarch, where Diana was a frequent guest. The princess also lived at the palace during her engagement to Prince Charles.

Diana, Princess of Wales Memorial Walk

The Royal Parks, London, United Kingdom
www.royalparks.org.uk/tourists/the-diana,-princess-of-wales,-memorial-walk
The Diana, Princess of Wales Memorial Walk leads visitors through the parks and past the buildings that were intimate parts of Diana's life in London. The 7-mile (11 km) walk is marked by plaques.

SOURCE NOTES

Chapter 1. The Fairy Tale

1. Andrew Morton. *Diana: Her True Story—In Her Own Words.* New York: Simon, 1997. Print. 124.

2. Ibid. 56.

3. Ibid. 125.

4. Anne Edwards. *Ever After: Diana and the Life She Led.* New York: St. Martin's, 1999. Print. 132–133.

Chapter 2. Becoming a Lady

1. Rosalind Coward. *Diana: The Portrait.* Kansas City, MO: Andrews McMeel, 2007. Print. 55.

2. Ibid. 54.

3. Ibid.

4. Ibid. 64.

5. Anne Edwards. *Ever After: Diana and the Life She Led.* New York: St. Martin's, 1999. Print. 53.

6. Bradford, Sarah. *Diana.* New York: Viking, 2006. Print. 29.

Chapter 3. Meeting Prince Charming

1. Rosalind Coward. *Diana: The Portrait*. Kansas City, MO: Andrews McMeel, 2007. Print. 55.

2. Anne Edwards. *Ever After: Diana and the Life She Led*. New York: St. Martin's, 1999. Print. 71.

3. Rosalind Coward. *Diana: The Portrait*. Kansas City, MO: Andrews McMeel, 2007. Print. 74.

4. Andrew Morton. *Diana: Her True Story—In Her Own Words*. New York: Simon, 1997. Print. 105.

5. Sarah Bradford. *Diana*. New York: Viking, 2006. Print. 40.

6. Andrew Morton. *Diana: Her True Story—In Her Own Words*. New York: Simon, 1997. Print. 45.

7. Ibid. 33.

8. Sarah Bradford. *Diana*. New York: Viking, 2006. Print. 65.

9. Ibid. 68.

Chapter 4. Diana, Princess of Wales

1. Andrew Morton. *Diana: Her True Story—In Her Own Words*. New York: Simon, 1997. Print. 115.

2. Ibid. 37.

3. Sarah Bradford. *Diana*. New York: Viking, 2006. Print. 74.

4. Andrew Morton. *Diana: Her True Story—In Her Own Words*. New York: Simon, 1997. Print. 34.

5. "Princess Diana's Engagement Interview." *YouTube*. YouTube, 11 Dec. 2010. Web. 20 Apr. 2012.

6. Andrew Morton. *Diana: Her True Story—In Her Own Words*. New York: Simon, 1997. Print. 37.

7. Ibid. 38.

SOURCE NOTES
CONTINUED

8. Paul Burrell. *A Royal Duty*. New York: Putnam, 2003. Print. 65.

9. Rosalind Coward. *Diana: The Portrait*. Kansas City, MO: Andrews McMeel, 2007. Print. 104.

10. Andrew Morton. *Diana: Her True Story—In Her Own Words*. New York: Simon, 1997. Print. 132.

Chapter 5. Motherhood

1. Anne Edwards. *Ever After: Diana and the Life She Led*. New York: St. Martin's, 1999. Print. 150.

2. Andrew Morton. *Diana: Her True Story—In Her Own Words*. New York: Simon, 1997. Print. 55.

3. Anne Edwards. *Ever After: Diana and the Life She Led*. New York: St. Martin's, 1999. Print. 179.

4. Sarah Bradford. *Diana*. New York: Viking, 2006. Print. 126.

Chapter 6. The People's Princess

1. Rosalind Coward. *Diana: The Portrait*. Kansas City, MO: Andrews McMeel, 2007. Print. 129.

2. Sarah Bradford. *Diana*. New York: Viking, 2006. Print. 150–151.

3. "Prince Charles: His Children, the Paparazzi, and Marriage to Diana." *YouTube*. YouTube, 27 Apr. 2011. Web. 31 Mar. 2012.

4. Andrew Morton. *Diana: Her True Story—In Her Own Words*. New York: Simon, 1997. Print. 61.

5. Rosalind Coward. *Diana: The Portrait*. Kansas City, MO: Andrews McMeel, 2007. Print. 177.

Chapter 7. The War of the Waleses

1. Sarah Bradford. *Diana.* New York: Viking, 2006. Print. 211–212.

2. "Annus Horribilis Speech, 24 November 1992." *The Official Website of the British Monarchy.* The Royal Household, 24 Nov. 1992. Web. 31 Mar. 2012.

3. Andrew Morton. *Diana: Her True Story—In Her Own Words.* New York: Simon, 1997. Print. 350.

4. "Philip, a Diamond Rock for a Queen." *Mail Online.* Associated Newspapers, 21 Nov. 2007. Web. 9 Apr. 2012.

5. "Princess Diana Interview End." *YouTube.* YouTube, 23 Oct. 2008. Web. 31 Mar. 2012.

Chapter 8. Queen of People's Hearts

1. Paul Burrell. *A Royal Duty.* New York: G. P. Putnam's Sons, 2003. Print. 266.

2. Rosalind Coward. *Diana: The Portrait.* Kansas City, MO: Andrews McMeel, 2007. Print. 294.

3. Paul Burrell. *A Royal Duty.* New York: G. P. Putnam's Sons, 2003. Print. 285.

Chapter 9. A Candle in the Wind

1. "Diana Princess of Wales Tribute." *YouTube.* YouTube, 2 Jan. 2007. Web. 31 Mar. 2012.

2. "Princess Diana's Funeral Part 17." *YouTube.* YouTube, 18 June 2007. Web. 31 Mar. 2012.

NDEX

ABOUT THE AUTHOR

Lisa Owings has a degree in English and creative writing from the University of Minnesota. She has written and edited a wide variety of educational books for young people. Owings lives in Andover, Minnesota, with her husband.

PHOTO CREDITS